ROMAN MYTHOLOGY

ANTHONY CLARK

ILLUSTRATED BY
MATT FORSYTH

Rourke
Educational Media

rourkeeducationalmedia.com

Before & After Reading Activities

Before Reading:

Building Academic Vocabulary and Background Knowledge

Before reading a book, it is important to tap into what your child or students already know about the topic. This will help them develop their vocabulary, increase their reading comprehension, and make connections across the curriculum.

1. *Look at the cover of the book. What will this book be about?*
2. *What do you already know about the topic?*
3. *Let's study the Table of Contents. What will you learn about in the book's chapters?*
4. *What would you like to learn about this topic? Do you think you might learn about it from this book? Why or why not?*
5. *Use a reading journal to write about your knowledge of this topic. Record what you already know about the topic and what you hope to learn about the topic.*
6. *Read the book.*
7. *In your reading journal, record what you learned about the topic and your response to the book.*
8. *After reading the book complete the activities below.*

Content Area Vocabulary
Read the list. What do these words mean?

blacksmith
fertility
harvest
hearth
loom
lyre
mortal
nymphs
tapestry
trident

After Reading:

Comprehension and Extension Activity

After reading the book, work on the following questions with your child or students in order to check their level of reading comprehension and content mastery.

1. *Name the 12 Roman gods and goddesses who live on Mount Olympus. What is the main responsibility of each god and goddess? (Summarize)*
2. *Where did the city of Rome get its name? (Infer)*
3. *Who was the queen of the Roman gods and goddesses? (Asking Questions)*
4. *If you could possess the powers of one of the gods or goddesses for a day, which one would you choose? Why? (Text to Self Connection)*
5. *Which planets in our solar system are named after Roman gods or goddesses? (Asking Questions)*

Extension Activity

After reading the book, choose one of the Roman gods or goddesses to further research. Find a myth, or story, featuring that god or goddess. Note how many other gods and goddesses appear in the same story. Find out if the god or goddess you chose to research appears in any famous artwork. See if you can draw your own version of the god or goddess based on what you learned in your research.

TABLE OF CONTENTS

Jupiter Statue
Bernini's Fountain, Rome

INTRODUCTION

Every culture throughout history has had its own dieties, or divine beings. The ancient Romans worshipped many gods and goddesses. Stories about gods, goddesses, and legendary heroes are called myths.

Some ancient Roman myths explained how and why things happened in the world. For example, lightning and thunder came whenever Jupiter, the sky god, hurled his thunderbolt down from the heavens. If a volcano erupted it was because Vulcan, the fire god, was angry. And **harvest** time came each fall thanks to the harvest goddess Ceres.

The Romans borrowed many of their myths from the Greeks. To make the myths their own, the Romans changed the names of the Greek characters.

Jupiter

IT'S ALL GREEK TO ME

Here are some important Roman gods and goddesses with their Greek names:

Roman Name	Greek Name
Jupiter	Zeus
Juno	Hera
Neptune	Poseidon
Pluto	Hades
Mars	Ares
Venus	Aphrodite
Cupid	Eros

THE GODS AND GODDESSES ON MOUNT OLYMPUS

Of all the Roman gods and goddesses, 12 stood out from the rest. These were the 12 Olympians. They lived on Mount Olympus and gathered whenever necessary at the palace of Jupiter. A real mountain in Greece, Mount Olympus was the mythical home of the gods for the ancient Romans as well as the Greeks.

Jupiter

Jupiter, the king of all gods, gained his crown by overthrowing his father, Saturn. As the god of the sky and of thunder, Jupiter controlled the weather. He wields a thunderbolt, and his animal is the eagle.

Juno

Jupiter's wife, Juno, goddess of marriage, watched over the Roman women. She wears a goatskin cloak, and she's often seen sitting beside a peacock. The month of June was named for her.

IN JUPITER WE TRUST

The symbol of the eagle holding a thunderbolt in its claws appears on some old Roman coins. The symbol was also used by the Roman army to honor Jupiter.

Neptune

Neptune, god of the sea, was one of Jupiter's brothers. Neptune wields a weapon called a **trident**. Whenever Romans won a sea battle, they thanked Neptune for the victory.

JUPITER'S OTHER BROTHER: PLUTO, GOD OF THE UNDERWORLD

Jupiter's brother Pluto didn't live on Mount Olympus. Instead, his realm was the underworld, the place people's souls were thought to go after they died.

Ceres (Summer)
(1718)
By Antoine Watteau

Ceres

Ceres, goddess of the harvest, taught the Romans about growing corn. Her daughter Proserpine was kidnapped and taken to the underworld by Pluto. In her grief over her daughter's fate, Ceres created winter. She makes the flowers blossom each spring when Proserpine returns to Earth to visit.

Mars

Mars, god of war, was the son of Jupiter and Juno. A moody god, Mars often liked to argue. Always dressed for battle and armed with a spear, he was the most important god to the Roman army. As they marched into combat, Roman soldiers prayed for Mars to carry them to victory.

The people of Rome thought of Mars as a kind of parent figure since he fathered Romulus and Remus, two important characters in Roman mythology. The month of March was named after Mars.

Finding of Romulus and Remus
(1612)
By Peter Paul Rubens

ROMULUS AND REMUS AND THE CITY OF ROME

Romulus and Remus were twins who were raised in the woods by wolves. When they were older, they defeated an evil king. According to the myth, after their victory, Romulus founded the city of Rome.

Minerva

Minerva, another one of Jupiter's children, wasn't born the usual way. Instead, it was said she sprang fully grown from her father's forehead. Minerva is the goddess of wisdom, trade, and the arts. She is also sometimes known as the goddess of war.

Minerva once took part in a weaving contest against a **mortal** woman named Arachne. Arachne won the contest, weaving a finer **tapestry** than Minerva. Jealous of Arachne's skill at the **loom**, the goddess punished the woman. Minerva turned Arachne into a tiny eight-legged creature doomed to spend its life weaving just to survive.

THE ORIGIN OF ARACHNID

Arachnid, the scientific word for spider, comes from Arachne, the very first spider. It's one example of the many words that came from ancient myths.

Minerva and Arachne
(c. 1645-1710)
By René-Antoine Houasse

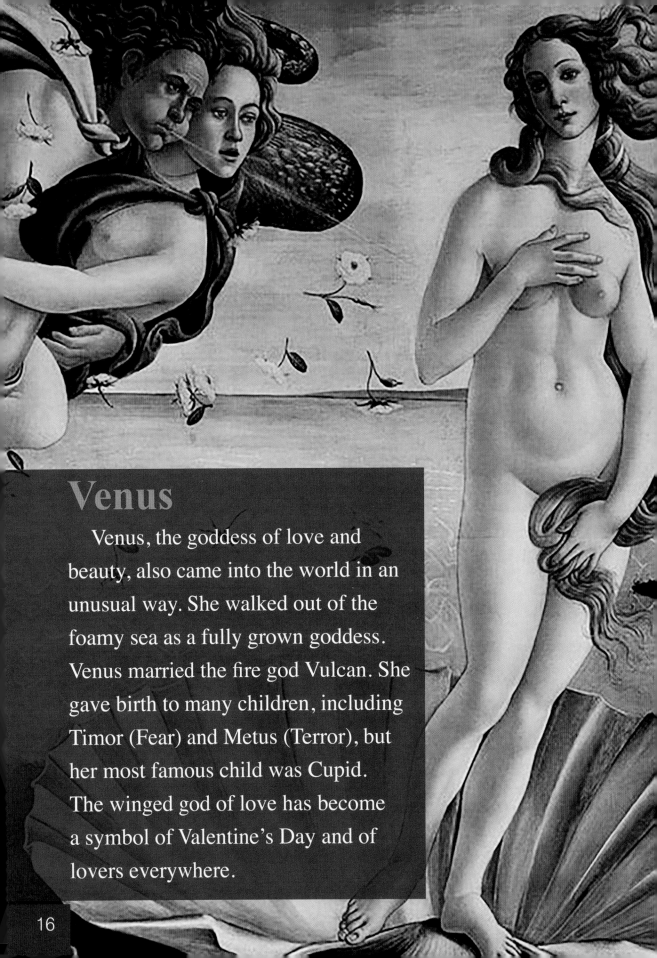

Venus

Venus, the goddess of love and beauty, also came into the world in an unusual way. She walked out of the foamy sea as a fully grown goddess. Venus married the fire god Vulcan. She gave birth to many children, including Timor (Fear) and Metus (Terror), but her most famous child was Cupid. The winged god of love has become a symbol of Valentine's Day and of lovers everywhere.

Venus is linked to multiple symbols, including the dolphin, the rose, the dove, the pomegranate, and the mirror. The popular goddess appears in many works of art. A number of paintings depict her rising from the sea in a clam shell. *The Birth of Venus (1484–1486)* by Sandro Botticelli is one of the most famous paintings of all time.

Vulcan

Vulcan, god of fire, was the craftsman of the gods. He's usually seen holding the hammer of a **blacksmith**. Vulcan had a tough life for a god. Most gods are handsome, but Vulcan was ugly even as a baby. He was so ugly his mother, Juno, tossed him off Mount Olympus into the sea. Vulcan was saved by **nymphs**, who taught him how to build things. But the long fall into the sea hurt him.

Vulcan had a hard time finding a wife. He finally married Venus, but she didn't always treat him well. Whenever Venus made him angry, Vulcan swung his hammer hard, making sparks shoot up from the earth.

FORGE FIRES

Vulcan made tools and weapons for the other gods. The word volcano comes from Vulcan's name. People once thought volcanoes were the chimneys of Vulcan's forge, or workshop.

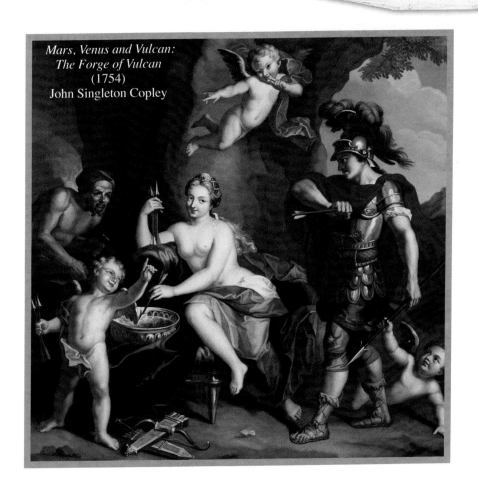

Mars, Venus and Vulcan: The Forge of Vulcan (1754) John Singleton Copley

Apollo

   Apollo was the god of truth, music, archery, and medicine. A son of Jupiter, Apollo was a very important god to the Romans. They believed he could bring them sickness or healing. Apollo is often seen holding a **lyre**, a musical instrument like a small harp. Sometimes he carries a bow and arrow.

Diana

Diana was Apollo's twin sister. Goddess of the moon and the hunt, she carries a bow and a quiver of arrows. She's often shown standing with hunting dogs or a deer.

DIANA'S AMAZING ABILITY

The goddess Diana had a unique power most humans would envy. She could talk to animals—and control them!

Diana the Huntress with her Two Dogs (16th Century) Italian

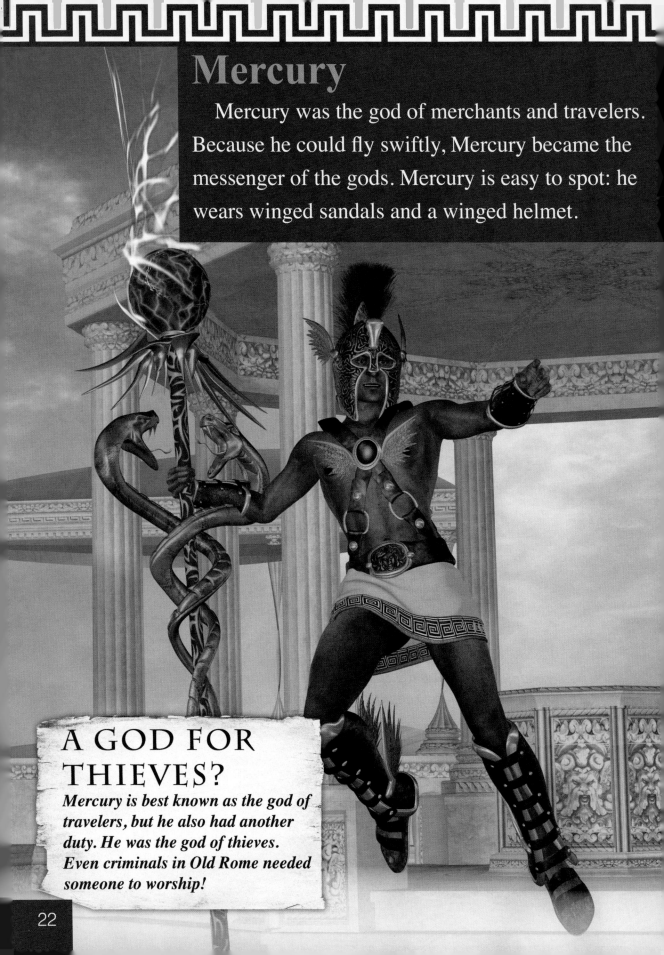

Mercury

Mercury was the god of merchants and travelers. Because he could fly swiftly, Mercury became the messenger of the gods. Mercury is easy to spot: he wears winged sandals and a winged helmet.

A GOD FOR THIEVES?

Mercury is best known as the god of travelers, but he also had another duty. He was the god of thieves. Even criminals in Old Rome needed someone to worship!

Vesta

Vesta was the goddess of **hearth** and home. Both Apollo and Neptune wanted to marry her, but she swore she would never marry. Whenever you see Vesta, she's usually near a donkey, her favorite animal.

Priestess of the Goddess Vesta making an offering (1887) Wood Engraving

OTHER GODS AND MYTHICAL HEROES

There were many other gods and goddesses besides those on Mount Olympus. Saturn, god of agriculture, was a very important god. He reigned throughout a peaceful time known as the Golden Age. His wife, Ops, goddess of **fertility**, was just as important.

Fearing that he would be overthrown by one of his children, Saturn ate some of them upon their birth.

The Muses were an interesting group of goddesses. All daughters of Jupiter, the sisters were goddesses of the arts and sciences. Each Muse watched over a different art form or area of science. For example, Clio was the Muse of history, Thalia of comedy, and the Muse of dancing was Terpsichore.

The Muses: Clio, Euterpe, and Thalia (1652-55) Eustache Le Sueur

WAITING FOR THE MUSE

The Muses were known to inspire poets and writers. Even today you sometimes hear writers and other artists say they're waiting for "the muse" to arrive.

Not all the characters in Roman myths were gods. Mortals, such as the brave female warrior Camilla, also appeared. When Camilla was an infant, her father, while fleeing his enemies, attached her to a spear, dedicated her to the goddess Diana, and hurled her across a river. Later in her life, Camilla led a band of warriors, including many maidens, into battle.

WARRIOR WOMEN

The Amazons were a mythical race of fierce female warriors. According to the myth, any males born into the tribe were either killed or sent away. The Amazons have their origins in Greek mythology.

The most famous hero in all Roman (and Greek) mythology was half-mortal. Because his father was Jupiter, the mighty Hercules was stronger than any pure mortal. As part of a punishment, Hercules had to complete 12 heroic labors or tasks. Among his heroic tasks, he captured some man-eating horses, slayed a nine-headed monster known as the Hydra, and seized the belt of Hippolyte, the queen of the Amazons. The last of the 12 labors was the most dangerous of all. For his final labor, Hercules kidnapped Cerberus, the fearsome three-headed dog-like creature that guarded the entrance to the underworld.

REMEMBERING THE ANCIENTS

The Romans built temples and monuments to honor their gods and goddesses. Remains of several temples and monuments are still standing today. Some of the best-known include the Tower of Hercules in northwestern Spain; the Temple of Jupiter, Juno, and Minerva in northern Africa; and the Temple of Jupiter in Lebanon. The Temple of Jupiter, in the Lebanese town of Baalbek, is the largest temple ever built by the Romans. The same town is also home to temples dedicated to Venus and to Bacchus, the Roman god of wine.

Temple of Jupiter

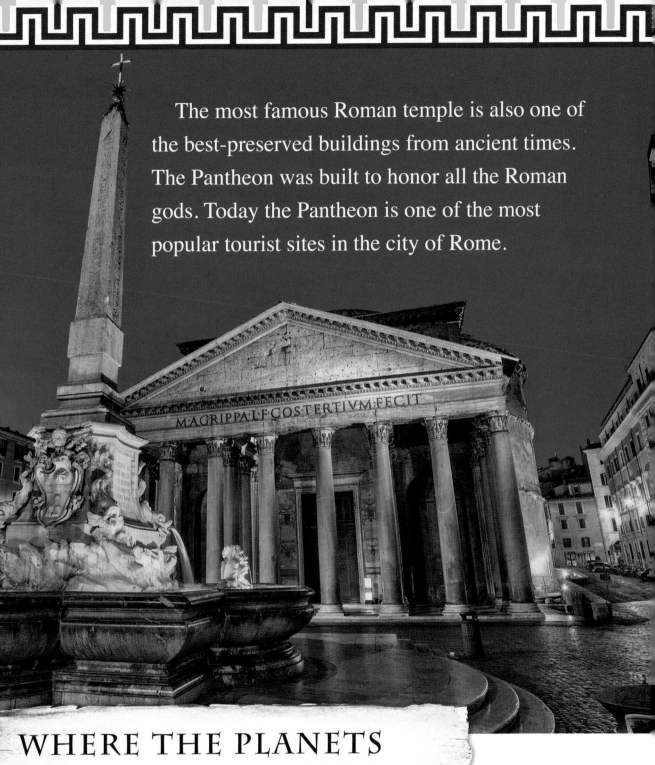

The most famous Roman temple is also one of the best-preserved buildings from ancient times. The Pantheon was built to honor all the Roman gods. Today the Pantheon is one of the most popular tourist sites in the city of Rome.

WHERE THE PLANETS GOT THEIR NAMES

Uranus and Earth are the only planets in our solar system not named after a Roman god or goddess. Uranus was an ancient Greek god, and Earth simply means "ground."

GLOSSARY

blacksmith (BLAK-smith): someone who makes things by heating and bending iron

fertility (fur-TIL-i-tee): the quality of being fertile, as in land that is good for growing crops, or a woman who can have babies

harvest (HARH-vist): the gathering of crops that are ripe, or the crops that have been gathered

hearth (harhrth): the floor in front of or inside a fireplace

loom (loom): a machine or device used for weaving cloth

lyre (lire): a small, stringed, harp-like instrument played mostly in ancient Egypt, Israel, and Greece

mortal (MOR-tuhl): a human being

nymphs (nimfs): in ancient Greek and Roman stories, beautiful female spirits or goddesses who lived in a forest, a meadow, a mountain, or a stream

tapestry (TAP-i-stree): a heavy piece of cloth with threads woven into it to make pictures or patterns

trident (TRYE-dent): a three-pronged spear, especially as an attribute of Neptune

INDEX

SHOW WHAT YOU KNOW

1. Where did the 12 most important gods and goddesses live?
2. Who did the ancient Romans thank whenever they won a battle at sea?
3. Who was Cupid's mother?
4. Who was the month of March named after?
5. What are the only two planets in our solar system not named after a Roman god or goddess?

WEBSITES TO VISIT

http://rome.mrdonn.org/myths.html

www.historyforkids.net/roman-mythology.html

www.talesbeyondbelief.com/roman-gods/roman-gods-index.htm

ABOUT THE AUTHOR

Anthony Clark is a teacher and professional storyteller who's published several books and dozens of stories and articles. He's written books about science, history, mythology, and business for adults and for children. He offers workshops in storytelling and creative writing. Clark lives with his wife near St. Louis, Missouri.

Meet The Author!
www.meetREMauthors.com

www.rourkeeducationalmedia.com

PHOTO CREDITS: Table of Contents: ©Flory; p.7: ©ZU_09, ©Samson1976; p.8, 10: ©Vuk Kostic; p.9: ©Universal Images Group North America LLC/Alamy Stock Photo, ©Yaroslaff; p.11: ©Art Reserve/Alamy Stock Photo, ©Nastco (background); p.13, 15, 25: ©Heritage Image Partnership Ltd/Alamy Stock Photo; p.14: ©Okea; p.16-17: Public Domain; p.19: ©John Singleton Copley; p.21: ©The Print Collector/Alamy Stock Photo; p.22: ©CoreyFord; p.23: ©Vector Goods, ©North Wind Picture Archives/Alamy Stock Photo; p.24: ©INTERPHOTO/Alamy Stock Photo; p.28: ©Anna Om; p.29: ©Noppasin Wongchum

Edited by: Keli Sipperley
Illustrations by: Matt Forsyth
Cover and Interior Layout by: Rhea Magaro-Wallace

Library of Congress PCN Data

Roman Mythology / Anthony Clark
(Mythology Marvels)
ISBN 978-1-68342-358-4 (hard cover)
ISBN 978-1-68342-893-0 (soft cover)
ISBN 978-1-68342-524-3 (e-Book)
Library of Congress Control Number: 2017931269

Rourke Educational Media
Printed in the United States of America,
North Mankato, Minnesota